ROCKY MOUNTAIN SYMPHONY

ROCKY MOUNTAIN SYMPHONY

The Sound, Colour and Moods
of the Canadian Rockies as portrayed by
a Poet-Writer and an Artist-Photographer

GB PUBLISHING

ROCKY MOUNTAIN SYMPHONY

Text by
JAN TRUSS

Photography by
GEORGE BRYBYCIN

Other photographic studies of George Brybycin:

THE HIGH ROCKIES
COLOURFUL CALGARY I
OUR FRAGILE WILDERNESS
THE ROCKY MOUNTAINS
BANFF NATIONAL PARK
JASPER NATIONAL PARK
COLOURFUL CALGARY II
WILDLIFE IN THE ROCKIES

Text Editor: Dorothy Dickson
Layout and design: George Brybycin
Project coordinator: Monica Jeannotte

Printed and bound in Hong Kong by
Everbest Printing Co., Ltd.
Colour separation by: Rainbow Graphic Arts Services

First Edition 1983

ISBN 0-919029-08-6 Hard Cover
ISBN 0-919029-09-4 Deluxe Edition

G B PUBLISHING
Box 6292 Station D
Calgary, Alberta,
Canada T2P 2C9

Front cover: Looking west from Cascade Mountain

About This Book

Profoundly beautiful, majestic, dramatic — this book is a tribute to a mountain man who has climbed, solo, well over a hundred peaks in the Canadian Rockies.
This publication reflects the very heart and soul of George Brybycin whose passionate love for and attachment to the Rockies have already resulted in the publication of seven pictorial books.

Mountaineer, naturalist, photographer, Brybycin is fast becoming a Rocky Mountain legend.

Prepared to spend long nights on desolate, wind-swept, craggy, high peaks, Brybycin has thus managed to capture the most beautiful and elusive visions of the Rockies at dusk, during the night and at dawn. Only one with his determination, unrelenting perseverance and deep feeling for beauty could seize such intimate moods, breathtaking colours and ecstatic moments of music in the Rockies as has Brybycin. He is rightfully called "a Poet with a camera" by reviewers and critics.

The adaptation in words of the Rocky Mountain Symphony was done by the internationally known poet, playwright and novelist, Jan Truss. Through Jan's understanding, soul-searching pen, her deep feeling and respect for the mountains and for nature, the essence of the photographs was captured and translated into poetic, musical, heart-warming phrases.

Listen to the powerful composition of the moods, colours and sounds of the Rockies.

Listen to the music of the heights.

Listen to the Rocky Mountain Symphony.

Sing the song of our mountains, they asked me. Sing the song of the Rockies. Find the words. Sing it gently. Fill it with loveliness. And while they were asking, I saw dark, jagged teeth, gnashing the sky.

I had to go out in search of the verses. There are so many and they sing so long. I had to listen to other singers who remembered lines they had learned from the massed mountain chorus that is robed in clouds. No simple lyric appeared. No single line of melody. These mountains are a full and mighty orchestra with an immensely complicated repertoire of staggering proportions.

And this great orchestration of ranges flings what it sings as far as peaks can reach across valleys and villages, foothills and highways, suburbs and cities, catching a vast audience, a following, a widely spread community of the Rockies.

This symphony of mountains and millenia is the time wrought harmony of upheaval, struggle and discord. It is a massive harmony scored in ice and rock on exposed craggy faces, and seared into the heart of man with body's toil, sweat and blisters.

The same almighty orchestra trumpets rage against protesting skies and strings a faint lullabye to a fragile alpine flower.

These mountains sing into a human soul until it is a giant soaring among them. These mountains loom and roar in threatening majesty yet lift minuscule man from heavy feet to anthems of glory. Or they drop him - a tiny staccato cry into a profoundness of silence with avalanches, pebbles in pools, lightning struck trees and discarded boulders.

This march, this dance, this anthem, this symphony of giants comes full-blooded, dynamic and marvellous, from the eclectic composer who reviles neither ancient nor modern, harmonic nor atonal, romantic nor brutal. Water's silver cascade orchestrates with the jet plane rising. Saws and mills harmonize with toads in marshes. The deep jewel of a glacier-gouged lake plays accompaniment to the wake of a smooth crimson canoe's reflection. Above the busy instrumentation of crowds and discord, above chattering squirrels and hustling grey jays, the lonely cleek, cleek, of the solitary climber's ice-axe beats its sharp time cleanly. Looping veins of transportation tracks and roads and corridors echo the savage cuts of nature's crevasses. The beaver flips a smack back to the cannon crack of the avalanches. And human voices diminish when a golden eagle cries.

This Rocky Mountain Symphony is a dramatic one, fully staged with a light show and an audience of stars. It is a multimedia production of such scale and magnitude that time itself is the continuo, time to infinity, time eternal, dispensing intervals of healing silence. Time holds the baton poised on colour and movement, on night and day. Time touches sunrise to waking.

Hush

Tune in to a pre-dawn concerto.

Silence holding peak to peak, snow to ice, to timeless crags. Farther than the imagination flows, a cresting sea of mountains billows, glinting below a sleeping sky.

Then - chip! Plink-plink-plink, through thin air.

A splintered fragment, a shed scale, flips and falls, falls, and falls across the half listening dreams of the climber bivouacked snug between a crusted wave of snow and sheltering wall of rock.

He misses a breath to listen.

Opens eyes on a streak of dawn that slices red from the fabric peak of his tent to the dark, long hillock of his mummy-bagged self. Illumination sudden, and brighter than Tiffany glass. First splendour of his day. Dawn distilled for his own illumination - touching with one small swift note the miracle of his soul.

He lies still, breathing slowly, comfortable with glory, marvelling at the gift. Layers and layers of silence roll in through tent walls until his ears buzz with the noise of it and the ticking of his watch is a metronome. Somewhere below a rivulet trickles, and falls, then cascades. The hushed roar rises, all one with the silence. And the climber is at one with all - harmonious.

The plain red tent glows gem-like, tucked into the rock and snowy crevice, touched by dawn, chariot of fire carrying one heavy-footed human climber into the lure and splendour of a mountain's day. His soul singing with the symphony.

Below in the plunge and spread of the stretching valley morning dreams of light. Darkness is paling. Birds whimper in veils of lilting mist like a section of tiny woodwinds tentatively tuning.

Dense shadows of crags ease their shoulders through mists of morning into deep shades of purple, mauves and mysterious greens. An early squirrel snickers. A ptarmigan shudders out from the sheltering skirts of a desolate crookedwood tree. One robin clears its throat, tests its pitch, then bursts its liquid notes in fluid and melodious call, thrilling the air with a lonely surge of love, a tenderness, a hope in waking. Sheep, pale layered notes on narrow music staffs drawn thin on the rock face, stand alert for sunrise sniffing towards meadows, while skittering pikas whistle among smoothed, fallen stones. Mosses clinging low in high places shimmer briefly with dew. A fragile flower quivers for one more rise of the curtain on the brilliance of her short and rare performance.

And here and there, each separated from the other by ridges and ranges, by rivers and valleys, and by peaks as yet only tipped with blush, the solitary humans wait. Rare as any endangered species, these solitary ones, more rare than Kirtland's warblers or peregrine falcons or the little swift foxes, these watchers of the dawn wait. Like worshippers hewn by the ages out of Celts and Stonehenge, they see the shrouds of the night luminous with great power and mystery. They wait for dawn as for the first dawning of the world. The mighty crags and forests wait. The very air itself seems to wait. A 'peace which passeth all understanding' hangs tremulous, touching all things. This dawn is the first morning. This mountain dawn IS the first primeval morning of the world, staggering the soul.

One solitary human sits, arms round knees, at the base of a lodgepole pine. Its hair is wet with morning drizzle and its eyelashes shine. It is wrapped roughly in an afghan, huddled against penetrating cold. The afghan is crocheted in a zigzag pattern that picks up the theme of striations in the cliff face that rises like an eternal wall above mighty trees it diminishes to stubble on a giant chin; a cliff face that was pushed up and folded like paper in the childhood of the world.

This human, a poet, could pass for a boulder broken from the rock face, a hunk of debris carelessly rolled by a giant hand. Wordless, the poet hugs the vision of dawning into the bit of warmth inside the afghan, to store it there. To store it until it settles into a pattern, until a melody of word takes flame, to capture in a few swift and winging notes the hushed and holy quality of morning's resurrection. Awed and wordless, the poet rejoices in the splendour when sunrise mixes mists, colours, crags, forests, barren sweeps of snow-pocked summer faces, cold limbs, and human emotions, in the cauldrons of mountain giants. The impervious giants themselves, lean and brood through mists and shades of shadows while the sun itself places on their flashy morning crown.

The poet fingers a cone, fruit of the lodgepole pine, knowing it gives up its seed, only opens up, in the inferno of forest fire. The human feels a metaphor in its fingers - and thinks it hears a poem waking from the mists.

Another solitary human leans among jagged precipices with a knee raised to make an awkward easel. This one, with narrowed eyes under cragging brows, with broad swift strokes of charred wood, and with the flat sides of chalk and pastel, labours intensely to catch shape and sound, movement and mystic majesty, in the bulging places of light and dark in the mist's pressure, and in the massive thighs of crouching mountains with pendulous crags. This artist struggles and labours to extract the essence of primeval morning through cold rock fingers onto raggy, rough paper.

There is might and brooding in the soft muted edges of pre-dawn. This is not prettiness. This is crouch, and push, and pressure, and crescendos of power, demanding equal power from the sketching fingers. There is a brutality in the beauty. How shall the artist convey the terrible force of these mountains and, at the same time, catch the uplift, the tremulous dazzle of wonder, the astonishment of a human soul?

The artist, one with those who wait, one with the worshippers and the contenders, struggles, labours, to produce one supreme expression, one fine fusion of charcoal, chalk, mountains, magnificence, dawn, and wonder, to catch the moving and majestic moment on paper, thirty six inches by twenty four. The surrounding mountains breathe quietly, pushing dawn towards morning. Today, as they did yesterday, as they did for every yesterday since creation, they will produce a priceless original. And, as though casually, they will throw in the full accompaniment of a rising orchestra to suit the mood.

If only the artist can catch it, catch the rare beauty, it can be shared with the millions who sleep in warm beds in close, small rooms, waiting for alarm clocks and bedside radios to awaken them to the business and concrete significance of a new day. A mystic moment of exultation from the mountains will, in the repeat and repeat of the one human vision, spread rejoicing from waiting soul to waiting soul in unending resurrections.

The campsite is way up the mountain, bulldozed into the forest above a glacial lake. A morning cloud rolls over the higgledy-piggledy village of campers in travel homes. Mists steam round license plates from a dozen cities. A girl called Melody, flattened on a top bunk under a roof with a boat on top, eases herself onto her stomach to see out of the narrow horizontal window. The forest is near, dark, fearsome with ragged juts of underbrush. It is gloomy, mysterious, dripping silver. She presses her nose against the window slit and turns her eyes up to where there is a glow, a pink coloured lightness luminous through the cloud, very high. Something awakens in her, some compelling necessity to lift her face into the veils of dawning, some memory passed down ages, brought across oceans by ancestors in sailboats peering through mists for beacons and lighthouses. With her clothes in her arms she climbs past sleeping bodies to let herself stealthily out into the shock of cold mountain air.

Silence presses suddenly, like a vise constricting. She recoils, tries to retreat. But already the closeness of the sleeping air is alien, rejecting. She gasps, closes the door, breathes in deeper the resin sharp sweetness of the pines. She pulls on her clothes, then unsure, vague as a dreamer in a solid world, tentatively moves among cars, holiday homes that vibrate with snores, and trash cans with bear-safe lids. Fear nags at her breathing. A mystical sense of aloneness such as she has never known before invades her. She is an explorer of an emptiness, discovering the land of solitude, where she moves in her own danger, floats with senses sharpened in clean and untrammelled emptiness. The cloud is wet on her hair, her eyelashes, the backs of her hands, as she stumbles onto a track through the trees going downwards steeply. She slithers on rough steps in the earth. She stamps her feet and chatters silly disconnected words to warn wild animals of her presence, in the manner it advises in the wilderness safety booklets.

Although her heart beats madly in her ears, she is not attacked. She goes on surviving, and arrives at the lake's edge which laps and swishes with a slow untroubled rhythm on a stony edge. She stands by the edge with the water running at her sneakers then receding.

The mist is white and rolling on the wideness of the lake. Forests brood, shadows in cloud. Mountain walls loom. And up on high, peaks are beacons washed with a glow of pink light. She stands with her face uplifted. A sensation of immensity absorbs and transports her. She grows with the wonder of mist and cloud, lake and mountain, and the luminosity, all inside her. She floats in revelation of herself large in the universe, while waves of morning rock their endless, timeless rhythm. The luminosity at the peaks turns pink to fire. Mist and cloud writhe, rise and roll, phantoms in the valley. In a cove, almost near her, a moose with heavy antlers treads with curves of rhythm slowly, ponderously, like a dream walker into a girl's morning. She feels privileged. Like God watching a miracle. She holds her breath.

Then a radio blasts an explosion of disturbance. The moose is gone. There are voices shouting to each other. More music. The mist is thinner. A green lake shows itself flat as emerald. Her feet are stiff and wet. She climbs back up the hill towards the noise and voices. But that delicate edge of fear that had made her an explorer, a discoverer, is no longer with her. She is back to ordinariness.

On the campsite a crowd with cameras is pointing and clicking at two black bears in a tree. It is not the same, not the same as it was when it was just herself alone with the moose by the water. Her parents shout, upbraid her for going off by herself. The girl holds something tight within her, something secret and precious, a sense of the immensity of herself learned from aloneness. In the lapping silence, among mists and giants with beacons at their peaks, she heard the melody of herself - a melody to whisper in her memory forever, luring to silences and dawns where the peaks are.

This man was a child nurtured and disciplined in other mountains, where the edelweiss grows. Now, he waits, a lean sharp shadow on a pre-dawn plain of ribbed and tortured snow, up among glaciers in the High Rockies. Alone as the first man on the Moon, he is a taut figure, commanding his landscape. For three weekends in a row he has made the same arduous climb to reach this place just below a summit, to camp here, to be on the spot for one particular aspect of a sunrise. He intends to catch it with his camera. He has glimpsed it before, a transient magnificence. Only glimpsed it from a wrong angle, just before it slipped away in the flow and rhythm of the ranges as first sunlight shimmered and glimmered across them. He stalks it like a hunter, waiting, alert, ready for the click, the finality of the take, the capture of the trophy. High above the sun, waiting in the gloom before light, he is awed and delighted again, as he is every new time, by the flood of first light, like the soft strings of a full orchestra, slipping across the peaks, muted, blushing, and glinting in flute and piccolo sharps and trills on snow places. The bulging mass and form he wants to catch, rests still in darkness. It is a colossal wind and weather sculpture of fungus forms hewn in heavy eons of crusted snow, swirled, humped, pocked.

He squeezes his fingers tight and hard into his palms to make blood flow up his arms and into his shoulders. The chill is in his bones. In the nights of waiting he is never quite warm, always chilled in those few hours in sleeping bag and red tent tucked under shelter of snow. Through the nights he hears the strange music of the glaciers - The Little Night Music of the crags - their rumbles, their crunchings, and their groanings. He always sleeps alert, keyed up for the assignation of the dawn.

Maybe this is the time he will catch the thing he has tracked down to its best position. If he doesn't get it today, he will be back next week, and the weeks after, until it is snared, captured.

The tripod is standing firm. The camera set.

He eases his toes in his boots, flexes his legs to encourage circulation. Flexes his fingers. Keeps the trigger finger warm. His exhilaration grows as the sun lifts, spreading glow and light and glint farther down the runs and trills of the peak, on peak, on layered peak. It is worth it every time, worth the labour, the cold, the blisters, the discomfort to witness the birth of the sun. It is love renewed. It is music for the soul.

Suddenly, he is one with the glow and the glory. An upshooting ray catches him like a mote in a beam, glorifies him in gold and prints his towering shadow in light above him on a mountain's shining face. Intoxicated in the high air, he shouts an involuntary halloo and raises his arms in a wide benediction. A child, a man, a god, he is the sunrise.

Then, the shine clouts his target. The snow takes fire. Its shadows blacken. Its pocks deepen. It is gold. It is glory. It is incandescence. Click - wind on - . Click - wind on - and click again. He has it. Had it at that precise moment of contrast and clarity when it stood only in the fire of the sun, in straight pure light.

Pause

The light show spreads. The peaks exchange reflections. The fungus-like snow sculpture slips into the general blaze-up of sunrise, its impressive solo performance over. But he has caught it.

Captured it. He sighs in contentment, and leans into the splendour of sunrise. Mutely, humbly, he wonders at the power of the glory; wonders who can live who has not come to birth with the sun.

Glaciers weep in the morning. Snows melt under hardened crusts. And waters slip and fall. Roundabout and in and out, among all the ranges of the vast symphony of the Rocky Mountains, the waters in their never-ending cadence link harmony with cacophony, melody with discord, time with eternity, scents with sunlight and shadows. Sometimes the water is no more than a shine on a grey rock face. Sometimes no more than a whisper under pebbles, or a hush like a distant sea in a deep fissure. In seep, glisten, droplet and in tears, down the waters come, from the heights to the valleys, from ice summits, through lingering snows, by the climber at the rock face, and the camper at breakfast, to the poet, the artist, the sheep safe-footing down to meadows, past hikers on trails, and campsites sizzling with bacon, and the fisherman by the waterfall. The waters gather their beat, their cadence, trickling and tinkling, swishing and splashing, spatting and spattering, gushing and bubbling, plunging and smashing, roaring and crashing, foaming and pounding, until they lose themselves in the roar of a highway, or are one in the flow of a river, or cradle themselves in the lap of a lake. As the waters fall their sounds rise up, up, up, through the layers. The everlasting hush of the waters rises gentle but mighty, a constant movement throughout the music of the mountains, persistent emotion in the rock score.

To have been by the waters in the mountains is to have known some moment of exultation, or peace illimitable when the self cried out I AM, I AM, and life and time knew a perspective.

Time in diminuendo lulls over peaks and waterfalls while humans sing out their solo I AM's - and a highway blares - and a railroad chugs on a precipice. Each and all the voices slip into the everlasting music of time small infinitesimal notes to add to the cries of the ages in the Rocky Mountain Symphony. A climber spread-eagled on a rock face, nose to stone, touches the bulge of a coral fossil under his fingers and hears loud again the whisper of seas before history reaching across three hundred million years. His own moment of delight adds its gasp to the mounting sounds of music, layer on layer, echo of ancient oceans.

Ghost voices of explorers hacking the first human pathway murmur through forests, and on a sheer climb the cries of ones who fell call again from the chasms. Such is the power, the grandeur and might of the Rockies, they keep past and present safe together in the closeness of their great womb. They keep their mystery and will let nothing diminish them. Their virgin valleys, seen suddenly from a climber's height or come upon as a surprise round a bend in a highway, call up cries of delight and joy. With unspoiled jewels of crystalline curving lakes, the march of forests and misty crags, these sudden visions flash those transcendent moments that make the human soul cry out, I AM. Yet, this Rocky setting is on such an almighty scale that a heavily settled valley with smoking chimneys, tamed orchards, fenced gardens and a tossed out litter of suburbia - all seen from a gravelled pull-off, planned and signposted by government department - can also evoke its cries of pleasure. These other human voices, add their tiny notes to the Rocky Mountain theme and continuity.

Whatever the valley or the vista, the voices of those first ones who saw it and were astonished echo through time. Voices of nomad hunters before the white man, voices of explorers, travellers, pioneers, are repeated and repeated in the imagination of the one and many who suddenly encounter the same visions again - again, for the first time, and cry out their astonishment at the miracle of gentleness and splendour.

While ancient seas sing in the high rocks of mountains, while waters fall, while humans cut and crash, blast and break and build, and renew their souls in the unspoiled vastness of the Rockies, the birds sing and the same moose treads down to his drinking. Those grey jays wheeoo-ing their insistent demands at this morning's campsite are the same jays, the Wesakichuks, who teased the first hunters in the valley before the horse, before the wheel. Grey jays zoomed in round the teepees where dark women laughed by morning smoke-fires, and Indian babies yelled their first cry to the mountains, their first resounding cry to the world, I AM.

These magpies on the meadows are the same magpies that clamoured round the lumber camps, stole meaty scraps from camp kitchens when the railroad when through and the first road was cut. The same magpies preening, long-tailed, glistening, laughing. The eternal magpies. The eagle dropping on its prey is the first eagle man saw here, and the same prey cries into the wilderness the first cry of fear. The same osprey flaps from the same nest, and a gay warbler flashes joy through the morning. This is the first morning.

Sing. Sing the song of the Rockies, they asked me. Find the words. Sing it gently. Fill it with loveliness.

I, the writer, waiting for words, walk down my pastures and, with feet soaked in dew, look to the mountains. The sun is dramatic across peaks and on glinting rock faces. The sky is very blue. A misted dawn silence lies serene across the forested valley, and all the wakings of the morning are hushed in the magnitude. All is loveliness. A happiness. Insignificant woman, in the shadow and radiance of these mountains, I am given a feeling of immense human significance and comprehension, and filled with awe. And I am a singer in the song of the mountains, catching my words from where memories dance with yesterdays among the ranges. This part of the song could go on forever, a divine Hymn to Loveliness. A soaring hosanna. A choral masterpiece with an infinity of tones and sections. Up to the clouds; their moods stretch out in soothing mists, in sunlit trills, in booms of amassed anger. And peaks themselves lilt like waves across an endless sea, or snap clappers at the sky; they rumble darkly, or scintillate like prima donnas with high winging clarity. Then valleys; valleys weep or mourn, lie lazy in sinuous lake-jewelled opulence veiling themselves in haze and muted langour. Fish jump-rings in opals, in emeralds, and in the amethysts of reflected skies, while water weeds sway above drowned upended mountains.

Breathe deep, take in the clear scent of snow. Snow in the heights in smooth fields of dazzle and purity. Snow ribbed across rocks like along celestial windows. Snow majestic, blown and weathered to sculptured form and set in fire of ice. Snow brushed on a glacier's wrinkled creeping. Snow flashing double images in the depths of a summer lake cradled in a mountain's elbow. And reflections themselves, as though one image were not enough to laud perfection, they try again, and touch a dazzling note to shimmer that reflection towards a human soul.

Then forests; almost too vast to find voice for, are so dense themselves with under-harmonies of roar, growl, snarl and shriek, bass, tenor and soprano. These forests, yet, are no more than moss in the valley, smooth, smooth, softly shushing. Streams. Water- falls. Narrow mountain torrents thundering in gullies loud with emotion. And meadows. Meadows singing out a quick, brilliant aria, in vivid flower-bright praise of avalanches that clapped them to the opening of their first performance. Avalanches sounding their crashing timpani as they clear the stage for meadows in the spotlight of the sun.

Above, a jet plane soars. It loops a silver clef across the sky, linking city towers to the long ridge of the Rockies. A railroad lays its silver track alongside a river. A highway cuts and curves. Rocky Mountain people huddled in cities watch the lure of these silver links with a longing that spans all seasons. Workers in office towers scuttle in the burrows of their corridors like those other mountain creatures, pikas, voles, ground squirrels, puffed up ptarmigan and labouring ants. They pop up at a thousand windows to sigh to mountains, dreaming of the week-end, of silences and shale scrambles, of water's hush and rock faces under the fingers, of trails, of lakes, of solitude and fellowship, of soul's exhilaration and re-creation.

The jet plane winging where their hearts are, casts its bird shadow as it flies. The shadow skims and wings across the whole great orchestration of rocks and ranges, a dark bird with the travellers inside it, seated in tidy rows. It crosses forest and avalanche, and the lake with the red canoe. It plays across the faint silver strings of highway, railroad, and river. It plummets down canyons, and rises to feather-kiss crone faces of prehistoric crags.

A passenger looks down. Sees the jet bird afloat in a crag-cradled lake. Imagines the passenger in the bird, in the lake, in the plane among the peaks, and laughs in a momentary revelation of harmony. Laughs. Drops a small new note of wonder into the ever rising glory of The Rocky Mountain Symphony.

Show us inside the great performance, they asked me. Show the parts and the harmonies. Show the music working its lure. Find the words. Find the words for the ineffable mystery, the lure of the mountains.

When the great dawn show is over, the mountains seem to rest. They bow their heads and tuck their shimmering fingers inside robes of purple or of blue. Often, from afar, it seems that a curtain has dropped on the Rocky Mountain performance. Closed, the jagged-edged stage sits flat against the sky across the edge of the world, waiting and mysterious. And yet, this darkened stage concealing muted instruments, lures humans to it as life-giving waters lure mountain creatures on twisting trails. Some, like varying hares who change their coats for winter, flash along with skis, or sails, or wings, with summer boats or winter snowshoes on their car tops. Short season players come lumbering with their houses on their backs. Cyclists come humped like bright bumble-bees to meadows. Scramblers come drawn to shale. The pom-pom beat of the highway marches them all towards the music of another Rocky Mountain day where already assembled players in many ranges tune up for the symphony of the afternoon.

On the road, early morning riders guide ponies through the dew and wave a merry flourish. A white-tailed deer leaps a fence and looks back startled. An Indian girl on the loneliness of the Reserve dances a private dance of joy, conducting her own music to the mountain morning. Freed flakes of shale and rocks skitter down the crowding slopes to join fir tree dwarfs, the natural bonsei that line the roadside among spiky grasses.

As the new day's players draw nearer, they scan the peaks. Loads of dreamers or doers, skiers, walkers or climbers, day trippers or over-nighters, the flyer, the fisherman, they scan the peaks to tune in to the colour and mood, tune in to the almighty rhythm of the dance of the giants against the sky. They all see that it is not the same dance, not the same piece they moved to last time. The lines and shadows have been subtly rearranged, their values changed by light and mist and shadow. These mountains never look the same two times over, never play it the same way they have played it before. Improvisation is the talent with which they astonish and stagger the senses. Every performance must be from a new score. And as the mountains play, the expression on their vast, time-creased faces is forever changing as they lift and lower them to the fiery and temperamental baton of the sun.

The sun, the resident daytime conductor, with a confidence drawn from the critical acclaim of generations of successful concerts, imperiously commands new presentations and interpretations. A lonely pinnacle, or a solitary tree stark against the sky, or a crystalline lake, or a thin falling torrent - can be unceremoniously called to solo loud and clear. A valley drenched in beauty will be called to a sudden wild crescendo then visibly restrained to hold itself down to a mere underlying harmony. Mighty forests are reduced to diminuendo while right before their eyes a single autumn branch is given a fortissimo fanfare. The sun will drowse for a jazz mellow interlude then stridently conduct a new concerto of thumping rock. It will become fey and hide its face behind some passing wisp of sky, then pettish - throw its baton to a bank of clouds, and - on occasion - to the falling smoke of a forest fire. When skittish, it can toss the baton to the peaks themselves handing them the power to make shadow plays of their own soaring heights and octaves.

Boom. Deep boom

Down

A looming peak conducts its weighty shadow darkly down a valley's depths to call up the mystery of the shades. From the heavy-shouldered marching forest it commands a slow, old chorus in basso profundo. The sounds come hauntingly, sounds from the underworld, from the dank and secret earth, to reach the sunlit cyclists resting on the wild climb of the road. These catch their breath as they stare in awe into the immensity of the hush of green. Something supernatural seems to touch their limbs, to threaten the bright notes of their summer clothes and gleaming steel. They mute their speech to whispers while they think of giants, of unknown monsters, perhaps of lurking civilizations lost to man in the enormousness of a Rocky Mountain thicket. The cyclists whisper in voices that believe in the Sasquatch, the most mythical monster of the Rockies.

Then, to break the spell, somebody shouts its name. The irreverent cry, a contrapuntal note, bounces round the peaks, then falls away into the hum of the ages. Again the strange power, the mystery, like a meeting with an almighty deity, strikes a note of uneasiness into the cyclists and the sunshine. They laugh. Their laughter rises, blithe arpeggios skimming through the air, rising merrily as they resume their climb.

Merrily

D ragonflies dive and skim touching pings of rings on the mirror of the lake. The resting paddle drips where, like a red willow leaf of an autumn remembered, a canoe slips over rings and ripples. The paddler perched on his own reflection floats across the deep blue sky among fluffy clouds to the lullabye soft snare-drum beat as waters lisp on meeting the bow. Mountains, afternoon drowsy, mildly watch the fragile vessel descending their heights and climbing their valleys. Sometimes they quiver then shake, tickled by the day that plays on their surfaces. Then they break the mirror sharpness of their echoes, and yodel at their own reflections.

Drifting to the mountains' song, to the gentle bobbing beat of the water, the paddler is meshed and woven in the lilting harmonies within harmonies. He drifts in valleys towards peaks that plunge before him to tangle fronded water weeds in their crowns of snow. He glides, one with it all, reflecting in reflections. His moment is trapped forever in the sun and the silence singing in the deep waters, trapped in the hollow in the heights, trapped forever to be reflected and echoed in a melodic lull in the eternal symphony of man in the mountains. And the moment is trapped in him to conjure forever - memory and longing.

The paddler drifts, drifts in the pastoral unity, until he is led into the white water song at the lake's outfall. The canoe makes of its wake a dazzle of fingers to pluck across harpstring ripples, as music and musicians rush to a fuller sound. The paddle pulls its own forceful beat while, foam flung high on the rocks sparkles diamonds in the sunlight - a flashing xylophone of bright sound.

Songs of the canoe, songs of the summits and the valleys, they sing out a plea. Share the mountain joy with all the people. Share the magnificence and the wonder.

So listen to the music of the mountains. There is peace unfathomable in it and glory. There is beauty and the towering strength of rugged endurance. There is healing for the troubled soul and there is exultation. Come, come, the photographer whistles like a Pan the Piper with a reed plucked and perfectly tuned in the wild places. He lays his sublime glimpses, views, visions, on smooth pages to transport us to where the air is clean and cutting on the face, and to where silence shatters the senses. He invites boots to know the crunch of brittle snow above the summer valley, and fingers to feel the sharp edges of rock, and the sinuous twist of the dark, dead branch where trees are scarce. Dance with me in the patterns of lake and rock and reflection, the Piper invites, showing sometimes how the camera catches a scene that is magically abstracted, like a ghost forgetting the substance of its body shows only the abstraction of its being. Come into the mists as well as into the clarities, come into patterns and the reflections, and know the glory firsthand. Bend to touch your cheek to a mountain flower.

There are governments who hear the songs, the pleas, and who join in serenades to the beauty of mountains with strings of trails and roads, with guides and guide-books, with stopping stations and scenic nooks made accessible in wild places. They try to play their part gently, to blend their twentieth century technical and atonal discords discreetly into wilderness harmonies; to open up for humble souls the hope of re-creation, and moments of glory when they can feel able to play a small part in the Rocky Mountain Symphony, and know the flow of its music like the lifeblood in their veins.

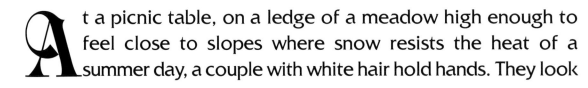

At a picnic table, on a ledge of a meadow high enough to feel close to slopes where snow resists the heat of a summer day, a couple with white hair hold hands. They look with pleasure from the blazing clarity of the peaks to the muted loveliness of the valley far below where a chain of massive lakes is delicate - from their lofty perch - as a child's necklace. All enclosing, the circling mountains hold summer safe in the valley, hold the forest small as terraced vineyards on their lower slopes, hold the nooks and indentations on the landscape where human flocks come to herd, and hold the rough clearing where the aging couple cling to present visions and to memories of other mountains, other years.

Together they breathe in the thin air that is warm with the day scents of spiky grasses. They smile when they hear the gurgles of water somewhere below singing up through the hushings of the treetops. Silent so as not to break the spell, the two spread an earth coloured cloth on the table, and unpack from a frayed wicker basket crisp rolls, good cheese, a foreign sausage. A wine glass for each is thoughtfully polished and the green bottle uncorked to breathe.

Close behind them a bare face of brown and grey sun-slaked rock rises, reaching for the summit. The woman and the man bend their heads back to look towards its crest, then they look down to the bulky time-smoothed boulders strewn about them onto the rough clearing below them where lanky fireweed has taken hold and blooms. Each of them remembers the roar of avalanches, the monstrous destroying thunder of the avalanche in nights when they lay half awake in tent or hut shelter waiting for dawn and warmth. Each hears again the hiss and scream, the violent music of the avalanche wind, and the roll of the torrents of rushing snow, the cracking, the snapping, the breaking. They remember the ice in their faces from times they raced on winged skis. They remember the rattle and the raging, the confusion and the settling debris, then the terrible quietness when it is done.

The unearthly quietness. Healing.

Wild roses bloom. They are very deep pink, struggling for place among tangles of weathered twig masses and fallen trees silvered by the years. Small blue butterflies dance in pairs over stunted willow bushes that have been chewed and pruned by elk and deer whose presence is everywhere.

The rocky clearing on the mountainside is a record of violence, of strength, and of the insistent grip of frail things clinging. There is peace here, a peace that comes from the heights, filling hearts with such beauty they think they will burst. Somewhere below the rock, a bird sings out one swift flow of melody. In unison the couple tilt their heads to listen, and in listening hear too the rasp of the highway that brought them here; hear highway music from the twisting strings of roads far below. The highway is a silver thread in the mountains, a flimsy thing, a narrow river in the river of time. It flings up its own beat and its bursts of throaty sound that merge into the hush and the glory of the eclectic chorus of day and time in the mountains. All the sounds are music, are the symphony, in the sun-warmed souls of an aging couple still singing from the heights - at a carefully placed picnic table.

Songs of the summits and the valleys, songs of the rivers and highways and the clinging railroad track, they sing out their plea. Share the mountain joy with all the people. Tell the people - Come.

The highway beckons with its signposts conducting loads of human families into sheltered spots where the mountains can hide them, enfold them, and feed the new sounds they bring into time's synthesizer. The families unload at tables and benches, some in hide-a-ways among ancient trees, some on the open space by the hum of the river. The cries and the shouts of the children call up to the listening peaks. Surprised as they were by the screams of the first mountain cat, by the first wild clashing to battling horns of mountain sheep in rutting season, or the first call of the Indian, or the first saws of the white man, or the first airplane above them, the mountains pause to listen, to let the new sound establish its own tone in its own small section of the orchestra. As the voices ring out and the children run merrily, and as radios clamour from a dozen discordant stations while the river gurgles, the mountains come closer with their skirts of forests drawn around them. In surprise they toss the jangled sounds among them through wisps of barbecue-tinted clouds. Rejoice and listen to the glad sound of our celebration - the humans carol with a compelling syncopation. In the security of their massed performance they are saved from the shyness and fear of a solitary song in the mountains. The welcoming banners of the signposts, and the roadways firmly pressed into the wild places under ancient trees by the flow of the river - they bring new notes, new sounds into the embracing majesty of the Rocky Mountain Symphony.

One child slips away from the happiness of the noise and the clangour. On the other side of the bridge, just a shout away from the site, he is alone in the bigger mystery of the softly breathing silence. The river pounds over washed boulders - but that is not a noise; it is part of the humming silence. A kingfisher dives headlong into the water, and deep into the child's imagination. He sees a wilderness fluttering with bright birds and he sees canoes gliding swift on the water under the paddles of men in fringed leather. He hears them singing. He climbs precariously across big rocks that raise dry heads out of the water, until he finds one that he can sit on, an island in the wash and flow of the rejoicing water. He is the men in the canoes singing; he is the kingfisher diving while the mountains watch. He is the little fish - caught by the mountains.

Caught to sing in the mountains.

Only the crunch, crunch of boots, sounds on a pineneedle trail. The forest is silent, taking a breath. Flecks of sunlight scatter small bright notes on the backpacks and bent heads of hikers ascending in single line. Time and timelessness is green and resin scented, shadowy and mysterious, humming in their heads while the close earth and the forest giants breathe. Their own breaths, their footfalls, pulse with the secret beat of the silence. There is a feeling of waiting, waiting. Then they are out in the sun, blinking while a trail guide softly tells stories of glaciers and while butterflies dance and insects buzz. Thousands of years, and thousands of years, words, words, dropping like old psalms onto the spears of the sedgegrass in the fen meadow. Softly time's continuo insists its melodies layer on layer, ghostly swishings of glaciers, stream, lapping lake, yearly sighs of folding leaves, from summer before winter, from the first summer of the world. Mysterious, romantic, the faint music of the ages surges in dreams, in the eyes of the hikers, lulling them into a harmony of whispers. Then there is a movement in the sedges and a spotted frog leaps. He leaps. His leap is as a sudden small crash of a cymbal into the intenseness of their silence. The watchers smile. Brought back to the roar of the mosquito clouds, they ease their packs for the next march on the climb through time and the long life-story of a single trail. A sandpiper flits before them teasing with its cries, and high above a red-tailed hawk screams. March of feet, scream of hawk, leap of frog, whisper of a sunlit afternoon - the symphony plays on.

A solitary hawk glides.

Humans with manufactured wings are poised on a precipitous ledge above cleared land. Wistfully they watch the hawk wing wildly then glide on its high faint scream.

Its cry is scattered like laughter among the hills while it coasts on air. Go - Go - a human cries. One leaps up and out, stretched between gaudy wings on fabricated frames. Cliff swallows flock from the rock face with a rising operetta of shrill twitters, then quickly wheel back to their nests continuing their fluting chorus as the monster bird with painted wings catches in the lift of the air and rises, a frail and lovely floating thing. Go - Go - the next hang-glider leaps, then the next, the next, and the next, till they hang and loop like a drowsy quintet of giant butterflies, admirals and swallowtails, tipping and tilting their rhythms and their colours to the bright baton of the sun. Each human bird lies stretched, the body in the butterfly. Icarus lives and glides, and rises in the updrafts. Fireflies, dragonflies, butterflies, the gliders make a ballet in the air, looking up to the peaks with dreamlike drifts, lifting and lilting above the green valley. Windsong is in their ears. They have found grandeur and splendour; they are the mountains' new wild birds, knowing the supreme freedom. They have found wings with which to soar, to sing, to solo in hills and glory.

Then the pollen scents of the earth rise up to whisper them down, down softly like butterflies drifting to the Lorelei sighs of avalanche lilies and bright mountain fireweed. Down softly they hum awhile, until the earth booms up with a green thudding drum. The wings crash and fold. The butterfly is transformed to a grasshopper rasping its legs and its scales. Then it is a slow cater-pillar as it was before, slow-crawling its way up the slope. Burdened caterpillars with their folk dreams calling them on, the hang-gliders labour uphill, a progression of tubas dreaming the silver trumpet sounds of flight. Up they go lured by the dream of flight. Cycle of life, cycle of the symphony, repeated and repeated. Reach for the heights, spread the wings, fly, soar, hit the high notes, solo, catch the eye of the sun, and lilt awhile. While the hang-gliders like heavy tubas blat to get to the top, swallows flash in curves shrilling a soprano chorus, and the hawk glides, flaps and glides, waiting to fall.

Down

The sun, before it bows out from another day's performance, reaches its long baton between the purple mountains to command mellow harmonies from the low-lying lake. In the glow of the golden spotlight the water shimmers with a gilded sheen. A barefoot woman in rolled jeans hushes a rowboat through the rise and fall of muskeg to a clear channel. The sun calls the hush to a slow and stately concert where all is in peaceful accord with the singing lap of the waters and the small gruff groans of the oars. Once on the open face of the lake the golden craft rests, rising and falling on the gilded glimmer. Fish jump, bright flashes, like plucked strings, pizzicato plops flicking rings and rings across the golden peace.

The resting oars drip. Pine forests drop upside down into the edges of the stretching lake, like dancers they contort themselves in ripples, and engage the mountains in a corrugated dance. Into the orchestration of hush and peace beavertails crash and spotted sandpipers cry across the muskeg. Two bears loaf on the shore beating a slow beat with their noses sniffing the air. Mosquitoes sing in golden clouds, and muskrats hurrying home to holes in the bank swim silver lines across the placid harmony.

Enough of small things, small sounds.

This Rocky Mountain Symphony demands a grander finale at the end of the day. The man with the camera is saturated with scenes of beauty, almost drunk with it. In a morning meadow he came upon a bull elk sniffing the flowers - or so it seemed; a bull elk with six points on his widespreading antlers grazing among new pine trees and fireweed and vetches. No matter how long he treads, climbs, almost lives in the mountains, there is always a feeling of being highly honoured when he meets one of the large beasts in its own home. Such meetings are rare, high-notes in the continuing high adventure.

All day he has been as one bewitched, lured to a lofty summit. It is always so. Enchanted by the rugged beauty and the amazing diversity of landscape and mood, he submits to the spell of the heights again and again. With his hopes set on the dazzle of the summit he left the meadows, paused on steep grass slopes to admire the expanse of the ranges riding away into the distance. He scrambled where the landscape was spartan and desolate pausing to look back where valleys and lakes wound their way into the distances of unspoiled loveliness. That's what casts its spell on him - always, the great distances of unspoiled loveliness.

Among the boulders above the scree and shale scrambles he stopped to talk to pikas, little creatures whistling and cheering the human giant among them. There were snow patches among the rocks and meagre vegetation where the pikas played. In a supreme state of happiness he works his way round the boulders, touches the weathered texture of the rocks - perhaps where no man has touched before. He thinks with pleasure of the scenes of the day and of the pictures he took; wonders if he will have caught the mood, the essence. There was one of the waterfall in a cleft, eerie as an artery to the heart of the world - so deep. He wonders - will he have caught the mysterious grandeur? The feeling he got in its presence?

Now he is almost to the summit that has lured him. He can see his way to the flat top where he plans to pitch his tent and stalk the loneliness of the moon. He stands to breathe deep, to survey the wonder of his world. It never stops - the glory of the wonder; the sense of freedom filling the soul. He knows he is bewitched, ecstatic, drugged, high on glory and loveliness. Before the hunting of the moon, he can stalk the sunset from the summit. He is always the hunter, stalking the moment which surpasses all moments, when all the instruments of nature en masse combine in a supreme expression. It is heady music, this music of the heights - so many rising crescendos of soul shattering purity. The silhouettes of the ranges stretch in undulating rows to some vague distant horizon. There is snow at his feet. The sun is off somewhere; has suddenly cast the baton to the looming clouds.

Clouds with darkening brows rise with authority until they form a higher, wider anvil summit, a dark inverted echo of the peaks. Perhaps the grand finale of the day, something suitably dramatic is about to sound out. With his camera ready for the moment more dramatic than all the other moments, he watches a distant anger cast its moody shadows and he fancifully imagines the pipe, piccolo, and flute trills of dancing sunshine silenced by deep haunting cellos calling for legato and pause, pause before a great, and an all surpassing burst of nature's expression. There are no words for what he expects. He awaits the almighty, the ineffable. The clouds spread and glower, and then, as though trying to outdo the sun's performance for the day, they snap a prima donna in - to dazzle the sky. Cracking and flashing, lightning makes its entrance reaching high with a swift piercing note.

The peaks light up in a vivid attention at that first clear call. Then, as lightning snaps the clappers in her fiery darting fingers, the mountain faces flash back encouragement to the devilish dance, seeming themselves to take fire as the demon leaps and contorts in a fierce tarantella. The man with the camera almost dances himself as he exults in the theatre of the distant storm. He is the rage in the peaks. He is the demon dancer, free in the heights where there are no barriers between body and soul. The mountains crouch over their drums watching for the instant to crash in on the clouds' rumbling bass chorus. The sounds rise, the lightning arcs and flashes more brightly. Then, with a crash, cymbal and drum, all the timpani, and all the percussion break in on the same wild note. The heavens tremble. The mountains throw the reverberation from peak to peak then roll it pounding down the valley. The camera clicks.

The camera clicks

He wanted to capture the glory and the noise of it, and the dancing fire that is kindled in himself. He wants to catch that moment mightier than all other moments when majesty is all powerful. He wants to capture the exultation and the wonder, to capture it for the smooth page of a book that when laid across the knees will share the mood, the great distances of unspoiled loveliness and the magnificent thunder of the rolling mountain symphony.

The lightning pauses, gathers itself for the next sequined flare.

Flash

Lightning in a spectacular downward glissando serrates a towering pine. Splits it with fire. A single flame sprung from lightning flashes through the dead arms and old needles of a single tree's long past winters, searing as it goes. It reaches up through a hundred summers of one tree's whispering green, then roars out into the air and the sky chased by a crackling fury of young flames it has spawned on the way. A sudden fiery autumn, swift as the frost in aspens, spreads a passing brilliance of orange and iridescent reds. Incarnadine tongues lick. The air explodes in a blue dancing rage. The Valkyries are riding and a thousand roaring demons rise and race across the ancient forest from tree to tree. Every instrument cries out in a sharp furioso. The heat is a fury. The red is an inflamed dragon belching black and evil smoke. The roar is an inhuman undercry in the symphony where gods and devils combine in rage. The burning air bellows and the earth cries out into the wind that rises from leaping flames into the passionate crescendo of the blaze. Mighty clappers clap as giants fall.

The peaks and the mountain shoulders lean and lilt in the kaleidoscope mirage of the heat haze; they shimmer, they nod, they bend, they undulate and mourn in the smoke cloud shadows. Finally they spread their limbs, their lakes and their precipices until they hold the raging fire safe in its place, confined. Rage and roar as it will, the forest fire is restrained to be no more than a bright fugue here and there in the ongoing concert; the same melody, the same instruments, as in all the forest fire fugues since time began. In among their black stumps and ashes soon one small white flower blooms then the fireweed marches in with jubilant fanfares of pink and purple. Lodgepole pine cones release their seeds - and as the phoenix rises from the ashes, so another theme rises, another triumphant air in the Rocky Mountain Symphony.

Smoke from the fire drifts in a hazy harmony, lying between peaks and down valleys. It darkens, it deepens, spreading its presence across wide sections of the orchestra and mountain chorus, until the sun hands the baton of the day to the smoke cloud. It is a strange visiting conductor, bringing a brooding quality, almost a sadness to the music. Certainly there is no fire in it, only a muteness, a greyness across the colours of the land, a hushed and shadowy waiting. And while the gloomily fuming conductor spreads a presence farther and farther, the sun retires to some ante-room in the heavens to borrow a magician's scarves to wave across the ultimate exit of the day. The beasts in the forests pant to the threat in the pulse of the music. The man with the camera watches the smoke cloud insinuate its unusual patterns on ice-etched faces, frown on green valleys, and transform glittering necklaces of lakes into grey cauldrons held in menacing giants' hands. The artist with swift wide strokes on a big canvas loosens inner angers in crouching planes of ominous brooding. Eyes search the mountain tops and the heavens for signs of rain.

Rain

The first spots of rain splotch tents and ping off metal holiday homes. They hiss on barbecue coals and explode where flames are raging.
Up there the peaks are gloomy, harassed by gathering ragged bands of jostling murky clouds. Jagged lightning whips up the anger of the sky. Such moods up there! Black and forbidding. The artist, the poet, the writer, the musician, see in the peaks the personification of all Mankind's brooding fury - or is it God's? They see Michelangelo, Beethoven, Wagner, riding the swirling clouds. The man with the camera watches the play of refulgent light between grey mountains where rain is falling like frayed veils of silver, dropping and lifting, soft and glowing as a water-colour, ethereal as heavenly music. And the music of the rain beats and surges, down, down, down on silver notes.

It splashes at high dusty faces and makes them shine. High above the trees it slakes the thirsts of sedimented oceans flung and folded against the sky. Sun dried and wind weathered, the rocks remember again the touch of the waves in the time before time when seaweed swayed, when clams and oysters shed their shells in the soft rills of their sand. Pebbles washed, and shale wet for a moment flip sips to thirsty moss as it clings for life. Cracks catch raindrops and strong mountain faces show their glistening lines. There's a splashing and a hissing. Crevices lisp and fizzle while gullies rush and swish. Grassy slopes shimmer. In the splashing, the slipping, the dripping, the rushing, the gurgling, and the pouring, the rain gathers force and flings itself into a full performance. It throws darts into waterfalls to be drowned in thunderous roar. It dashes itself into a fierce oblivion in crashing cascades. It slices at straight precipices only to trickle into meagre pools where sheep may safely drink. It ruffles smooth lakes until they are pocked and broken and it drops teasing freckles on green-eyed pools.

A damp person, a poet, sits arms round knees, in the doorway of a tent, watching for words in the swish of the cascade of the mountain rain. The sibilance is enclosing - every string in the orchestra vibrating with sustained and dampened sound. From the sky to the peaks to the fall of ledges to the valley the sound splashes and hisses. It pelts the tent and thuds into the sparse grass, kneading up mud. It fills the treetops and turns pine branches to spouts, and broken boughs to grimacing, sputtering gargoyles. Tree bark glistens, some glows green. Raindrops ping off boulders like sprays of fallen stars. Lakes lie in wide leaves that support tiny flowers, then spill over. A squirrel shelters by a tree trunk with its paws above its head. The sky, the trees, the rocks, the earth, all hiss and roar in the swell of the rain - the rising strings of the falling rain. The tent is a waterfall. The trees are a waterfall and the towering heights are a downpour. The mountain is a waterfall smelling green to burst the heart. The poet, hair streaming, is inside the waterfall, is the rain and the rainsong in the mountains.

Sing the song of the mountains, they asked me. Find the words. Sing of the ineffable mystery. Sing it poetically - the song without words that goes on forever.

There is blue under the mist after rain. And all the birds suddenly burst out singing. A raindrop on a sedgegrass spear is a world complete, shimmering and reflecting. Hanging mists are luminous. An ethereal light hangs softly, gentle in the air between the washed hues of clouded hills. The man who was nurtured in other mountains treads carefully at the edge of a fragile meadow. Small pines brush against him and fireweed, the same fireweed as in that earlier home, brushes his hand. It strikes a note of nostalgia or homesickness - perhaps the merest touch to a triangle - in the Rocky Mountain harmony. The man who was a child in other mountains touches the narrow leaves and is pleased with the misty music of this day - and with the unfathomable, magic harmony the mountains bring.

After the rain, the climber at the summit above the sun sees across a celestial sea of swirling mists and floating peaks. There is an inner glow of refulgent light lifting the mountains above all clouds. The soul seems to soar free. The labour of the climb, the blisters, the cold, the discomforts are all as nothing. The climber floats among Gods and as he soars he knows why Man climbs mountains. In the rare high air, heavenly choirs are singing with an awesome and marvellous clarity.

In another high place, Himself with his camera watches, willingly bewitched by the glow, the radiance, the harmony. A rainbow arches across the sky, diadem to an ermine cloaked afternoon. There are no words too extravagant for catching the glory - the never-ending glory. Rocks steam, mists roll across glimpses of very green valleys. Lakes lie blue, serene and lovely. Beauty flows, mysterious, trailing illuminated veils off to infinity. Himself watches a golden eagle hang in the rainbow. Its cry scatters among the rocks, bouncing, reverberating. Silver glowing mists undulate in valleys and steam across the rilling peaks. Himself watches the magnificence of the images, contemplating how they arrange themselves to achieve the transcendent mystery, the breath-taking power. It is the total luminous mystery he wants to click and capture; something bigger than the sum of the images. He is the hunter waiting. He studies the interaction of light and cloud, of mass and colour, of silence and clattering sound and, with the patience of the possessed, plans ways and means to lure the haunting mood and beauty into his Rocky Mountain Symphony.

The baton is taken gently by a pale moon which soon brings out the whispers of bats' wings. The mysterious owls swoop in with their short solos. A wolf's howl quavers and is echoed and re-echoed through the gathering shadows. Coyotes with thin voices sing out ghoulishly for the coming of the night. The coyote choir grows as valley responds to valley and peak to peak; the curtains of coyote callings are drawn round the edges of the symphony of darkness. Trees are brittle, motionless. In the high meadows flowers are all closed. The insect requiem for the day has gone.

Colonies of campers make huddled villages of lights, very small starglows in the landscape of the vast and blackening night. Forests and mountains gather round them, closing in to watch the flicker-dance of human shadows grown to giants against the light of cooking fires and lanterns. The passing river, so hushed and gentle in the light of day, now gushes out a sinuous presence, roaring and splashing with a formidable insistence. Lakes slap around shores and moan with notes that lay quiet under the baton of the sunshine. Moths, ghosts of the night, haunt lanterns and candles. Smoke from cookfires hangs low in hovering wraiths. Children are kept close in the lighted groups as night-time wilderness crowds in closer. A bough breaks, a tree falls, a boulder rolls - and the little edge of human fear is dispelled with uneasy

43

laughter. Someone shines a light into the crashing darkness - a pinprick in the awesome secret places of the untamed night.

Himself, the man with the camera, has watched the flamboyant sun topple over the last of the peaks. The sky has moved through navy blue shades to pitch black, catching as it deepens the scintillating concert of millions of stars. He watches the moon climbing in the sky. Far, far below, glow worms of traffic define an earthly highway while he sets his camera to record the orbing pathways of the stars. He is in the magic world of star-glimmer and moon-glow. He can almost hear the stars twinkling in the sky as far as the illimitable horizon where the moonlit-starlit ranges flow like a heavenly sea. The tired body weary from the day's climb, dreams of sleep but in the high mood of the thin air the mind will not rest. The moon will not be quiet. It calls up with its brightening baton the big night music of the universe and directs it into the tiny orange tent, filling it with all the glory of ethereal splendour. Cold is in the bones - but the heart and mind are compelled to go on and on joining in the rejoicing of a new night's splendour in the Rocky Mountain Symphony.

I, the writer, waiting for words to find the music of the night, walk out into the forest. It is very dark and resin scented. This forest is all the forests of the mountains, breathing a mysterious silent music that pulses to the swishing of my feet in pine needles and last year's dry leaves. I am the thread in a phantom melody, my sound a brush across a snaredrum, my heart a metronome. Here and there the sky flings down a spattering of moonlit notes onto the earth. The white bark of a deciduous tree glimmers a long silver note at intervals. Young boughs swoosh breathless passing calls and old twigs snap. Mice make quick little runs and dashes. A porcupine scratches a long dry note on the forest floor. There's the pleep, pleep, of the rabbit feet pizzicato. A great cat screams a quick solo into the trembling darkness. Far above, the treetops shush, and shush. I stop. Against the beat of my heart the largo of the forest sounds out its dark mysterious night music and coyotes raise their voices.

Out in a clearing, moonlight falls white as snow.

The chord of fear that vibrates through the dark forest diminishes. The beauty of the open night sings with a million stars in the soaring dome of the sky. The moon brings the lone cry of the wolf and the ragged choir of the coyotes into tune. But the mountain air is cold. The night air of the Rockies always whispers of winter, whispers the long memories of long, long winters.

Under the white moon the valleys remember the smoothness of snows and call up the songs of the skis. When the cross-country skis break trail, the new snow, like bellows made from veils, lisps out crushed sounds and lays itself out - parchment for the score of the winter symphony. Twisting and looping, following frozen rivers and wisping over deer paths, the ski-trails swish around the valleys and lilt with a myriad human notes. Jolly in bright toques and gloves, these human notes pipe their little flutes and trills like bright and sparkling baubles into the cold serenity of white and far-reaching harmonies. The peaks are snugly clothed and mountain shoulders hunch thick collars round white-lined crag faces. The forests are wondrously weighted with blossoms of snow which, when they fall, call the shush of their cadence into the white-robed concert of winter.

On steeper slopes the downhill skiers flash in quicker bursts of melody adding sweeping curves and spirited dances. The wrapped mountains with radiant faces nestle round these brilliant pockets of performance in resounding ski-villages where vivid little orchestras try out new instruments such as chugging ski-lifts, roaring skidoos, and clattering ski-rentals. But the songs from round the blazing fires at mountain inns and remote ski lodges are like the old song sung round lonely campfires when snowshoes printed the first ornate notes of Man's earliest scores in the mountains. Songs rise up from the new fires to mingle with the old songs of the explorers and history, all a part of the very short movement of man in the vast and rolling symphony of the Rocky Mountains.

Under the silver moon of summer the white waterfall and the flowing river remember the ice silence of their sculptured winter. A small breeze waved up by the baton of the moon to dust snow-powder on the faces of crags remembers bravura performances when as a mighty wind it roused the ranges to raging furiosos. Then, it drove snow screaming down valleys. It howled in canyons and made tempests in towering trees. It flew in the faces of ripples and waves as they raced on the waters and it held them still for the ice to grip. In a frenzied duet with the snow it buried lakes and built mountains in the meadows. It whipped up a swirling, a demonic world of white.

The sleeper at the summit is restless and chilled. The white moon of summer shines an ethereal illumination through the nylon tent. The tent slaps and shudders like a sail on the sea. It tugs at its guy-ropes; it strains at its pegs held by night ice. The wind, ebullient, effervescent, bursting, rushes round peaks banging on rock faces, dancing its crazy and erratic dance from boulder to boulder, from summit to brow-beaten summit. It beats and buffets the tent entreating it to take off, to fly, to wing, to soar in the rising glory of windsong and almighty freedom of the night. The sleeper, now wide awake, lies at the heart of the tumult, is one with the tempest, the battering and the howling. In awe, in fear, he wonders when the crazy wind will toss him, tent and all, to lift and rise in the mad, mad music - then drop him, a falling cadence to cry a lone lost cry through the symphony of the night.

A falling cadence

For another climber the mountain day has been long. Himself, the singer of the lone song, is weary and drunk on beauty. He has known dawn and sunset and the splendour of the day. Like the first man he has wandered, climbed and stumbled, towards the lure of the first summit of creation. He has wandered through movement after layered movement of rare ascending music, where every dissonance has been transmuted and bewitched into soul-stirring harmony. Soft mists and green valleys sing along with necklace lakes in his head. The pandemonium of discords that thudded through him as he wandered with fear among abysmal mazes of treacherous crevasses is now the sweet melody of challenge met and conquered. Now, the star song of the heavens is too loud for his weariness. Night calls his body to sleep.

Sweet melody

On this climb there is a shelter ahead; a climber's hut. When Himself sees a glow on the snow and some flitting dance of shadows, he thinks he is hallucinating in the high air. Someone is before him in the cabin. A thin line of smoke rises from the chimney above a snow-puffed roof. Tracks on the trail have no claws.

Snow has formed thick overhanging eaves to make a fairytale cottage, and light from the small window falls like a sprinkling of pale gold across sculptured drifts. It is very pretty; a fantasia on a gingerbread theme, full of delicate melodies to end the day. Himself opens the door and is called in to a hearty welcome. Two climbers with their gear stacked by the wall are busy with a pan on a black stove. Warmth and aromas of food are a greeting, and the thick log walls are mellow in the dancing lights on candles. Soon there are tales of the climbs of the day and a spreading of food on the sturdy table. Then, as though to offer a humouresque to the heady music of the day - in the pan on the black stove there is lobster. Lobster. Carried frozen from seas far below, the lobster has come home to the ancient seas in the heights of the mountains. The little cabin in the peaks laughs.

Under the high baton of the moon a silver harmony slips across the majestic sleeping mountains. The same moon that called up the tides on prehistoric seas conducts the eclectic concert of a new night. Rugged crags coruscate with silver jewels and lakes glint back to the stars. Tempest tossing silver clouds mingle their clangour with the hush of sleeping forests in time's slow continuo. The everlasting hush of silver water rises while glaciers crack and melt. Mankind, grouped or solitary, is tucked into the silver tents of the night among the memories of the mountains' unfolding ages, while the silver highway and the railroad track shimmer their pathways to lure new generations to the challenges and the glories of the Rocky Mountain Symphony.

The moon reflects itself in a breathless lake. The photographer catches the moments, the rare and lovely moments of his Rocky Mountain Symphony to share with those who sleep warm in their beds. And the northern lights shoot across the sky to add a final fanfare of magnificence.

Jan Truss

Plates

Poetry of the mountains. Tangle Ridge (3,001m) reflected in the Sunwapta River.

South slopes of Mt. Wilson (3,261m) reflected in a mountain tarn. Banff National Park.

Kananaskis River and Mt. Kidd (2,958m) in the Kananaskis Range.

Kicking Horse River and the Van Horne Range. Yoho National Park.

Athabasca River and Mt. Christie (3,103m). Jasper National Park.

Vermilion and Ottertail Ranges, Mt. Goodsir (3,562m) viewed from Storm Mountain (3,161m).
Kootenay National Park.

The Monarch of the Canadian Rockies - Mt. Robson (3,954m). The rugged south face. Mount Robson Provincial Park.

Morning image of Mitchell Range in the central-east part of Kootenay National Park.

The steep, rugged slopes of Mt. Fay (3,234m), by Moraine Lake. Banff National Park.

The Fortress (3,002m). Kananaskis Range. Kananaskis Country.

Mt. Saskatchewan (3,342m). Saskatchewan River. Banff National Park.

64

Mt. Goodsir (3,562m) and glaciated Mt. Owen (3,087m) as seen from Mt. Stephen (3,199m). Yoho National Park.

West craggy face of the Cathedral Crags (3,073m) as seen from Mt. Stephen (3,199m). Yoho National Park.

Idyllic morning scenery of Mt. Robson and the Robson River. Mount Robson Provincial Park.

Hector Lake and the Waputik Group photographed from Mt. Hector (3,394m). Banff National Park.

The Carthew Lakes from Mt. Carthew (2,621m) in the Clark Range. Waterton Lakes National Park.

Bow Range dominated by Mt. Temple (3,547m), veiwed from a snow cave. Kootenay National Park.

Sunrise over Mt. Assiniboine (3,618m), photographed from Cascade Mountain (2,998m). Banff National Park.

Looking south from Storm Mountain (3,161m). Banff/Kootenay National Parks.

Picturesque Lundbreck Falls on the Crowsnest River, east of Crowsnest Pass.

The Fraser River winding through canyons and narrows. Mount Robson Provincial Park.

The Saskatchewan River cuts its way through a rocky gorge two kilometres from its source, the Saskatchewan Glacier.
Banff National Park.

Austere beauty of mountain morning. Lawrence Grassi Hut, a southern sentinel of Clemenceau Icefield. Mt. Clemenceau (3,658m) dominates the horizon.

The north-west face of the Canadian Matterhorn - Mt. Assiniboine (3,618m) viewed from Magog Lake.
Mount Assiniboine Provincial Park.

Mt. Assiniboine (3,618m). Lower part of the North Glacier which feeds Magog Lake.
Mount Assiniboine Provincial Park.

Hector Gorge, Vermilion River and Mitchell Range as seen through fish-eye lens.
Kootenay National Park.

Cavell (left) and Angel Glaciers cascade down the formidable north side of Mount Edith Cavell (3,363m). Jasper National Park.

Swaddled by mist from Wapta Falls, the Kicking Horse River. The area is lush with flora and abounds in fauna. Yoho National Park.

Annual cross-country ski race "Telemark" on Lake Louise in the shadow of Mt. Victoria (3,464m). Banff National Park.

As the tracks show, a skier narrowly escaped a snow avalanche from Mt. Fay (3,234m), by Moraine Lake. Banff National Park.

Early morning autumn fog over Maligne Lake. Jasper National Park.

Lake Minnewanka and the Fairholme Range viewed from Cascade Mountain (2,998m). Banff National Park.

A colourful sunrise on Mt. Bourgeau (2,931m) photographed from Mt. Norquay (2,522m). Banff National Park.

Reflected in Maligne Lake, an opalescent moon clears Le Grand Brazeau Range and its formidable glaciers. Jasper National Park.

Dance of the sun on the Bow River near Canmore, Alberta.

The Athabasca River under a cold −30°C. Jasper National Park.

Climbers on the lower slopes of Mt. Lefroy (3,423m). Mt. Victoria (3,464m) provides the background. Banff National Park.

North glacier of Mt. Sarbach (3,155m). Top of Mt. Chephren (3,266m) in the background. Banff National Park.

Egypt Lake (left), Mummy Lake (centre) and Scarab Lake, viewed from Pharaoh Peak (2,711m).
Banff National Park.

Close to the summit of The President (3,138m), looking north-east. Yoho National Park.

Southern slopes of The President (3,138m) looking south. Yoho National Park.

Saskatchewan River and Mt. Forbes Group. Banff National Park.

Mysterious Robson River. Mount Robson Provincial Park.

Located near Egypt Lake and Pharaoh Peak (2,711m), a cozy and warm hut is a home away from home for hiker, skier and climber. Banff National Park.

Mt. Rundle (2,999m) and Vermilion Lake. Banff National Park. Light, colour and crisp air combined to create the mood in this photographic composition.

After a day of hard skiing, what could be more pleasant than to share a fire and drink tea or wine with a group of friends?
Egypt Lake Hut. Banff National Park.

Located high on the south side of the Bow Range, the Fay Hut is a base camp used for the climbing of Mts. Quadra, Fay, Little, Bowlen and Allen. Kootenay National Park.

Mt. Robson (3,954m). Highest peak in the Canadian Rockies. Mount Robson Provincial Park.

Athabasca River near Jasper. Mt. Christie (3,103m) in the background. Jasper National Park.

A cold morning on the Athabasca River. Jasper National Park.

Rawson Creek. Kananaskis Provincial Park, Alberta.

Sea of peaks. The glory of a sunrise viewed from Storm Mountain (3,161m). Banff National Park.

Glacier of Mt. Coleman (3,135m). Banff National Park.

Glacier of Mt. Sarbach (3,155m). Banff National Park.

The Ramparts. Lush alpine meadows in the Tonquin Valley. Jasper National Park.

Mount Rundle (2,999m), one of the most photographed mountains in Canada. Banff National Park.

A solitary climber's camp on Panorama Ridge (2,824m). Banff National Park.

Spring thaw on Cameron Lake. Waterton Lakes National Park.

The awakening of spring in Kootenay National Park. The Vermilion Range in the background.

The emerald waters of Egypt Lake with the reflection of Pharaoh Peak. Banff National Park.

The forces of nature at work. Cobb Lake. Kootenay National Park.

----and three times in a row, I climbed this mountain in mid-summer and three times, it snowed up there---
Mt. Edith Cavell (3,363m). Jasper National Park.

Sunset in Kananaskis Provincial Park, viewed from Mt. Rae (3,219m).

Smoke from a burning forest in the Vermilion Range. Kootenay National Park.

A display of nature's grandeur witnessed from the summit of Mt. Carthew (2,621m).
Waterton Lakes National Park.

Emerald Lake and reflection of Mt. Burgess (2,599m). Yoho National Park.

Sparkling waters of Amethyst Lake and The Ramparts. Jasper National Park.

Morning glory over Lake Minnewanka and the Fairholme Range. Banff National Park.

Night scenery of the summit ridge of Mt. Edith Cavell (3,363m). Jasper National Park.

Emerald-green waters of Marvel Lake. Banff National Park.

West side of massive Mt. Wilson (3,261m), as viewed from Mt. Coleman (3,135m). Banff National Park.

Witnessing the birth of a new day from Storm Mountain (3,161m). Banff/Kootenay National Parks.

N

Sunset over a vast expanse of the Kananaskis Country. Lower and Upper Kananaskis Lakes photographed from Mt. Sarrail (3,170m). Kananaskis Provincial Park.

Glacier and Kaufmann Peaks (right), Mt. Epaulette, White Pyramid, Mt. Chephren (left) as seen from Mt. Sarbach (3,155m). Banff National Park.

Humble signs of the awakening of spring on a mountain tarn. The Mitchell Range. Kootenay National Park.

*From its source in Egypt Lake, Pharaoh Creek rushes down to merge with the waters of Redearth Creek.
Banff National Park.*

Protected by The Rockwall, Floe Lake, the jewel of the Vermilion Range.
Kootenay National Park.

A rich palette of colours, moods and shapes. The Upper and Lower Consolation Lakes and Mt. Babel viewed from Panorama Ridge (2,824m). Banff National Park.

Electric storm phenomenon over Mt. Christie (3,103m) and the Athabasca River. Jasper National Park.

A silvery moon glowing over the Montana Rockies. Viewed from Mt. Carthew (2,621m). Waterton Lakes National Park.

Rapids on the Kicking Horse River. Yoho National Park.

Glowing sunset sky reflected in Medicine Lake. Jasper National Park.

The rising sun gently touches the cornices of Observation Peak (3,171m). Banff National Park.

The Ball Range, east of Stanley Peak. Kootenay National Park.

Mt. Burgess (2,599m) reflected in Emerald Lake. Yoho National Park.

Nature used gentle pastel colours to paint this mountain landscape. Lake Maligne. Jasper National Park.

Peace and serenity in the snow-clad solitude of the mountains. Mt. Kitchener (3,505m) and the Sunwapta River. Jasper National Park.

Looking down from Pharaoh Peak (2,711m), the name Mummy Lake came naturally to the mind of A.O. Wheeler, a pioneer, surveyor and mountaineer who looked upon this oddly shaped lake and gave it its name. Banff National Park.

Spring thaw on Vermilion Lake. Mt. Rundle (2,999m) in the background. Banff National Park.

Nigel Peaks (3,211m) and the Saskatchewan River on a winter morning. Banff National Park.

A blending of sounds, shapes and colours. A view from Cascade Mountain (2,998m), looking West.
Banff National Park.

The heavily corniced south summit ridge of Mt. Temple (3,547m). This mountain is located a few kilometres south-east of Lake Louise. Banff National Park.

The massive north-east face of Mt. Ball (3,312m) aglow in the rising sun. Photographed from the ridge connecting Stanley Peak with Storm Mountain. Shadow Lake on the left. Kootenay/Banff National Parks.

Merlin and Castilleja Lakes viewed from Mt. Richardson (3,086m). Banff National Park.

Summit ridge of Mt. Richardson (3,086m), Mt. Hector (3,394m) in the background. Banff National Park

Mysterious, challenging, inviting. The Cathedral Crags (3,073m). Yoho National Park.

Morning mist over the Bow River valley and Castle Mountain (2,766m) viewed from Panorama Ridge. Banff National Park.

A sea of mountains looms in the morning mist. Looking south from Storm Mountain (3,161m). Banff National Park.

A new day is born. Vast panorama of mountains captured from Storm Mountain (3,161m). Banff National Park.

The sun sinking behind Mt. Goodsir (3,562m), a giant of the Ottertail Range. Kootenay National Park.

Beautiful, severe, formidable and challenging. Winter image of the north-east face of the Black Pyramid, better known as Mt. Chephren (3,266m). A guardian of Chephren and Waterfowl Lakes and the Mistaya River. Banff National Park.

Partly frozen Moraine Lake in late June. Example of the very short summer season in the Rockies.
Banff National Park.

Winter barely relinquishes its grip on the northern high slopes allowing less than five months of growth to the vegetation. Yoho National Park.

Austere beauty of glaciated mountains. The Columbia Icefield viewed from Mt. Athabasca (3,490m). Jasper National Park.

Fed by the mighty waters of the Daly Glacier, Takkakaw Falls (380m) plunge into the Yoho Valley. Yoho National Park.

Sunset over a wintery scene at Medicine Lake. Jasper National Park.

Mt. Quadra (3,173m) and golden larch trees. Banff National Park.

Consolation Valley in the grandeur of autumn. Banff National Park.

Mystery of the night. Moonlight on Maligne Lake. Jasper National Park.

Mt. Robson (3,954m). Mount Robson Provincial Park. A mountain of many faces, moods and challenges. The microclimate created by this mountain makes the region a zone of heavy rain and snowfall which feed numerous glaciers, torrents, rivers and lakes in the surrounding area. On the south side of the mountain, a lush rain forest flourishes.

The Rocky Mountain Symphony unfolds from the summit of The President (3,138m). Mt. Carnarvon (3,040m) on the left. Yoho National Park.

Poetry of the Heights. A heart-warming view of the Valley of the Ten Peaks at sunrise, photographed from Mt. Temple (3,547m). Banff National Park.

A grand panorama of mountain landscape. Morning glory from the summit of Mt. Temple (3,547m), facing south. Banff National Park.

St. Nicholas Peak (2,972m), a northern sentinel of the Wapta Icefield. Bow Hut is visible in the centre. Banff National Park.

Sunrise witnessed from the summit of Mt. Richardson (3,086m). The Wall of Jericho on the left. Banff National Park.

Emerald waters of Edith Lake. Pyramid Mountain in the background. Jasper National Park.

Lake Oesa, located above Lake O'Hara, a gem of Yoho National Park.

A very cold October night was spent on the summit of Mt. Coleman (3,135m). Banff National Park.

The Royal Group dominated by Mt. King George (3,422m), seen from Mt. Sarrail (3,170m). Kananaskis Provincial Park.

Morning image of the rugged east slopes of Cirrus Mountain (3,267m) viewed from Mt. Coleman (3,135m). Banff National Park.

A welcome sunrise brings back the colours and warmth after a long dark night. Mt. Coleman (3,135m). Banff National Park.

The Alpine Club of Canada's Elizabeth Parker Hut. Yoho National Park. Sharing, respecting and showing consideration for others help to create a friendly atmosphere in the mountain huts, thus assuring a pleasurable and memorable experience to the alpinists.

Photographer's Notes

Music has been within me since birth. Whether it be the hum of a city, the rushing of a mountain torrent, the howling of the wind on a high ridge, even "rain drops falling on my head", all sound-impressions are music to me.

Many classical pieces were created by composers who were overwhelmed by the majesty of the heights. Music has been significant for me for so many years that one day, I decided to synthesize my activities and try to compose my own Symphony of the Heights, using a camera instead of musical instruments. The heights and their magnitude were to be the orchestra, the weather-mood the conductor and I, the viewer-listener, the composer. Thus started my odyssey.

The most inspiring, awesome, although frightening, symphonic movements I have experienced are those I heard on the summits of high peaks. The whining of the wind, gnashing of the ice from a moving glacier, the rumble of snow and rock avalanches, galvanizing strikes from electric storms, the deafening sound of heavy rain or hail, the doleful howling of blizzards, create a cacophony of sounds never to be encountered elsewhere. Had Beethoven experienced such magnitude of sound, can it be imagined the symphony he would have created from them?

After this metaphorical prologue, I would like to present to you the photographic and mountaineering aspects of my project.

When my selection of photographs for this book was nearly completed, I noticed I had not included a Jasper National Park landmark, Mt. Edith Cavell (3,363m, Plate 127). This mountain is monumental, challenging, so I set out to 'compose' pictures of it. But the disdainful mountain did not see it my way. She was unkind to me, not once, but three times in a row.

Yes. This is right. Three times I climbed Cavell in mid-summer and three times, she was rude enough to call rain and snow to hide herself from me. I never even got a glimpse of the Angel Glacier below her peak, shut-in by clouds as I was. On my third climb though, the full moon chased the heavy rain long enough for me to produce the mood on Plate 135.

The dilemma of being able to take good photographs in the mountains is illustrated by the fact that though at times I took two weeks of holidays in the Rockies, ten days were mercilessly spent in wet and misty weather.

A studio photographer commented he was bewildered by the fact that it took me an average of two to four years to collect enough material for an outdoor pictorial book. He said it would take him two months. I suspect he does not quite understand what is involved in photographing mountains. From my personal experience, I can vouch that only one out of four trips may bring the desired results. Otherwise it rains, snows, is foggy or smoggy.

A mountain photographer is faced with a very difficult although magnificent environment. Canadian winters need no description. It must be remembered that on high elevations, severe conditions prevail most of the year. Some photographs in this book seem rather warm, even poetic. This is an illusion created by colour and light. The reality is not quite so poetic.

At sunrise, the wind-chill factor on a high peak often creates temperatures of −20°C or lower. During winter, it could go down to −50°C or lower.

It is then that I face the greatest challenge of all: to struggle out of the relative warmth of my tent before sunrise and 'muster up' my artistic mood.

Another aspect of mountain photography worth mentioning is the photographer-mountaineer combination.

Artists are not necessarily in good physical condition and mountaineering requires that one be in the very best shape. Is this why good pictorial mountain publications are usually the result of the combined efforts of many contributors? This harsh and rugged environment is extremely difficult to cover. In books using aerial photographs, the warmth, the inner feeling and the personal touch of the photographer with his subject are missing. Such books are acceptable, of course, but the viewer does not feel the intimacy of the photographer with his environment. I am proud of the fact that all of my photographs are the result of my climbing and hiking on foot.

The variety of wilderness subjects is limitless and forever offers me enjoyable discoveries. High altitude landscapes are my favourite subjects. Mountains are my friends. When I sit on a high summit and let my eyes scan the horizon, I am pleased to recognize most of the peaks in my field of vision. When viewing a summit of a known mountain from a different angle, I am fascinated to discover the new face of an old friend.

Doubtless, were I producing books only for myself, all would be on high altitude landscapes. But my love of the heights is not necessarily shared by all book lovers, so I chose to present a selection of milder subjects as well. I want my book to be attractive and interesting to as wide a circle of nature lovers as possible.

When one has climbed solo well over a hundred peaks in the Canadian Rockies as I have, one is bound to encounter various adventures, sometimes really hair-raising experiences. When bush-wacking in remote wilderness areas, I have met nose to nose with grizzly bears. Many times I have had less than desirable trail companions including wolves, a raging bull moose in rutting season, a mountain lion and many, many black bears.

Setting out to climb high peaks alone is often a way to experience much more than one expected. I still recall with a shudder a dramatic incident on Mt. Ball (3,323m) in Kootenay National Park. I approached this huge pyramid from the west, via Haffner Creek. Nightfall caught me on the glacier about 300 vertical metres from the top. As my aim was to spend the night on the summit, I pushed on in the dark, cutting step after step in the 55° ice-wall. But a chilling wind soon developed and tiredness caught up with me so I looked for a suitable spot to pitch my bivouac. Unable to find one, I had to continue to hack my way up. Finally I reached a small icy ledge just large enough to hold my tent. The night was warm and I took a well deserved rest. The next morning, the persistent sound of rain on my tent told me there was no tremendous sunrise out there but still, rain or not, I decided to continue on to the summit.

I stuck my head out of the tent and stopped dead, a strange tingling running under my skin for there, under my nose, gaping up at me hungrily, was a huge black hole. That icy ledge where I had pitched my camp turned out to be the very end of a large crevasse covered by 25 centimetres of drift snow. Any unfortunate move, I knew, could cause this fragile bridge to collapse, dislocating me 200 or 300 metres down to cold eternity. I stepped out of my tent with extreme caution and folded the contraption in record time.

The rain made my progress on the glacier so slippery and dangerous that it was in vain that I tried to make any headway. I had to give up. Once again a tremendous effort at high risk had yielded no reward.

I have experienced similar close calls many times but they never discourage me. I would rather die 'on duty' as it were, doing what I love than lessen my efforts because of the danger. My philosophy is: treat the mountains with all due respect and they will tolerate your intrusion.

But not all is tragedy on my trips. There are also humourous sides to this kind of adventurous life. In late September last year, when I camped on top of The President (3,238m) in Yoho National Park, the night was very cold but sparkling clear. A perfect night to photograph the sky and stars in motion. I judged my photo would require roughly a one hour exposure. I set my camera out in the cold and crawled into my sleeping bag. It had been a long rough day and I found it difficult to stay awake. Tiredness overtook me. I awoke in the middle of the night with the vague feeling there was something I was supposed to do but not being sure what it was, I went back to sleep.

While I slept, trouble was slowly brewing. A quiet, heavy snow started falling, burying my camera under over 20 centimetres of white fluff. What kind of picture of the night sky did I get this time? You guessed it: a 'slightly' over-exposed (8 hours!) photo. If ever I wondered why my cameras last me only two to three years, well by now, I should have the answer!

Later on that winter, I repeated the 'star in motion' photo idea but this time in much more comfortable circumstances. As I snuggly sat inside the Elizabeth Parker Alpine Club Hut in Yoho National Park, I left the camera to suffer alone outside for one hour (Plate 200). You will notice the dashes in the track of the stars. This is the result of the passing of small clouds between the camera and the stars during the exposure time.

To succeed in any field you must first love your subject. The Rockies are my love. Could I ever stop mountaineering? No never.

What does mountaineering do to one? Well, to conquer a mountain is to overcome one's fears and weaknesses, thus it means to conquer one's self. Blizzard, rain and sunshine, frost and wind, all combine to carve a mountaineer's face, to crystalize a strong character. The beauty of the mountain lives on, reflected in the conqueror's eyes.

So I will continue climbing, exploring and photographing mountains for as long as physically possible. My outdoor escapades give me a tremendous feeling of health and wealth. I am rich in beautiful experiences and adventures no money could ever buy. My wealth needs no security men to guard it, it is in my heart, deeply enshrined in my soul.

George Brybycin

The Authors

JAN TRUSS is an award winning Canadian novelist and playwright. Her short stories have been aired on CBC in Canada and BBC in England, and been published in both commercial and literary magazines. She is published by Atheneum, and Harper and Row in New York, by Douglas & MacIntyre, Lebel, Alberta Heritage, and Playwrights' Co-op in Canada. She is acquiring an international reputation as a writer for young adults. Her home is a small bushland farm in Water Valley with views across forested foothills to the Rockies. Her works are varied, ranging from plays for the very young to a libretto for an opera, SILVER CITY, about the ghost town at the foot of Castle Mountain, west of Banff. She has done commissioned works for educational publishers and most recently the descriptive prose text for ROCKY MOUNTAIN SYMPHONY. Alberta landscapes supply her settings. A novel, BIRD AT THE WINDOW, winner of the First Search for a New Alberta Novelist Competition, is set on the prairies, while JASMIN, a novel for young adults is set in Water Valley, north-west of Calgary, and A VERY SMALL REBELLION takes place in lumber country west of Edmonton.

GEORGE BRYBYCIN is one of Canada's foremost mountain photographers. Mountains and their solitude are his world. "Humans must live in harmony and in a close relationship with nature to understand its laws and cycles", he says.

George has spent much of his adult life travelling throughout the Canadian and American West in search of the beauties and challenges offered by this fabulous mountainous region. He has climbed solo well over a hundred peaks in the Canadian Rockies.

Born and educated in Europe, he grew up in the pervasive intellectual atmosphere of the old continent.

His sensitive nature was enriched by extensive travels in Europe and around the world. Although a sophisticated city man, contact with mountain wilderness as a child marked him for life as a mountaineer and nature lover.

George is the author of nine pictorial books and possesses what could possibly be the largest one-man collection of photographs of the Rockies and western wilderness in Canada. His dream is to keep producing books depicting the grandeur and fragile beauty of nature, thereby helping man to find his roots and appreciate his destiny.

Index

ROCKY MOUNTAIN SYMPHONY
ROCKY MOUNTAIN SYMPHONY
ROCKY MOUNTAIN SYMPHONY
ROCKY MOUNTAIN SYMPHONY
ROCKY MOUNTAIN SYMPHONY
ROCKY MOUNTAIN SYMPHONY
ROCKY MOUNTAIN SYMPHONY
ROCKY MOUNTAIN SYMPHONY
ROCKY MOUNTAIN SYMPHONY
ROCKY MOUNTAIN SYMPHONY
ROCKY MOUNTAIN SYMPHONY
ROCKY MOUNTAIN SYMPHONY
ROCKY MOUNTAIN SYMPHONY
ROCKY MOUNTAIN SYMPHONY
ROCKY MOUNTAIN SYMPHONY
ROCKY MOUNTAIN SYMPHONY
ROCKY MOUNTAIN SYMPHONY
ROCKY MOUNTAIN SYMPHONY
ROCKY MOUNTAIN SYMPHONY